D0910423

S E L E C T E D
P O E M S

David
Malouf

SELECTED
POEMS

Angus&Robertson
An imprint of HarperCollins*Publishers*

AN ANGUS & ROBERTSON BOOK
An imprint of HarperCollinsPublishers

First published in Australia in 1991
Reprinted in 1992
CollinsAngus&Robertson Publishers Pty Limited (ACN 009 913 517)
A division of HarperCollinsPublishers (Australia) Pty Limited
25–31 Ryde Road, Pymble NSW 2073, Australia

HarperCollinsPublishers (New Zealand) Limited
31 View Road, Glenfield, Auckland 10, New Zealand

HarperCollinsPublishers Limited
77– 85 Fulham Palace Road, London W6 8JB, United Kingdom

National Library of Australia
Cataloguing-in-Publication data:

Malouf, David, 1934–   .
    Selected Poems

    ISBN 0 207 17280 3

    I. Title

A821.3

Cover illustration by Louise Tuckwell
Typeset in Palatino by Midland Typesetters
Printed in Australia by Griffin Press, Adelaide

5   4   3   2
95 94 93 92

CONTENTS

At My Grandmother's

An afternoon late summer, in a room
shuttered against the bright, envenomed leaves;
an underwater world, where time, like water,
was held in the wide arms of a gilded clock,
and my grandmother, turning in the still sargasso
of memory, wound out her griefs and held
a small boy prisoner to weeds and corals,
while summer leaked its daylight through his head.

I feared that room: the parrot screeching soundless
in its dome of glass, the faded butterflies
like jewels pinned against a sable cloak;
and my grandmother, winding out the skeins I held
like trickling time, between my outstretched arms;

feared most of all the stiff, bejewelled fingers
pinned at her throat or moving on grey wings
from word to word; and feared her voice that called
down from their gilded frames the ghosts of children
who played at hoop and ball, whose spindrift faces
(the drowned might wear such smiles) looked out across
the wrack and debris of the years, to where
a small boy sat, as they once sat, and held
in the wide ache of his arms, all time, like water,
and watched the old grey hands wind out his blood.

Epitaph for a Monster of Our Times

The age admires precision
and this man was precise,
a passion for names and numbers,
they say, his only vice;

a kindly man, with blue
and inoffensive eyes,
a public servant, slightly
smaller than lifesize,

who sat at his desk, a slave
to files and paperclips,
while children died and cities
burned at his fingertips;

a Caligula by proxy,
stiff-collared, dispassionate,
whose crablike hand recorded
number, name and date,

using the regulation
form, the official quill,
to sign with equal flourish
death warrant, laundry bill;

an organisation man
par excellence, whom we
need only convict at last
of gross efficiency.

The Year of the Foxes

for Don Anderson

When I was ten my mother, having sold
her old fox-fur (a ginger red bone-jawed
Magda Lupescu
of a fox that on her arm played
dead, cunningly dangled
a lean and tufted paw)

decided there was money to be made
from foxes, and bought via
the columns of the *Courier Mail* a whole
pack of them; they hung from penny hooks
in our panelled sitting room, trailed from the backs
of chairs; and Brisbane ladies, rather
the worse for war, drove up in taxis wearing
a GI on their arm
and rang at our front door.

I slept across the hall, at night hearing
their thin cold cry. I dreamed the dangerous spark
of their eyes, brushes aflame
in our fur-hung, nomadic
tent in the suburbs, the dark fox-stink of them
cornered in their holes
and turning

        Among my mother's show pieces—
Noritake teacups, tall hock glasses
with stems like barley sugar,
goldleaf *demitasses*—
the foxes, row upon row, thin-nosed, prick-eared,
dead.

    The cry of hounds
was lost behind mirror glass,
where ladies with silken snoods and fingernails

3

of chinese lacquer red
fastened a limp paw;
went down in their high heels
to the warm soft bitumen, wearing at throat
and elbow the rare spoils
of '44; old foxes, rusty red like dried-up wounds,
and a GI escort.

Stars

The stars have so far to go
alone or in harness
across a window pane.

Hour after hour tonight
I've journeyed with them, steady
the waves of your breath.

Dark space between our beds;
on the table a full tumbler
splits the light of stars

to stars, or floats
a column of dead water,
dead sky. From centuries

off, out of the reign
of one of nineteen pharaohs,
a planet's dust, metallic,

alive, is sifted down,
hovers in a bright
arc upon your cheek.

Miraculous! I lean
across the dark and touch it,
you smile in your sleep.

How far, how far we've come
together, tumbling like stars
in harness or alone.

The Music Lesson

'Keep time, keep time!' My fingers vaulting over
the barlines of a Bach Prelude were caught
by the flick of the metronome, the index finger
of Sister Martin wagged, as if the air
had somehow disobeyed her, swirling past
the snag of her squared nail to the window where
the afternoon began. Her boot, round-toed
and black on the carpet's worn Axminster roses
kept time (I smelt its blacking) and my flight
through hedges thorny-thick with notes took off
at the window ledge. Crack, crack! My knuckles jarred,
caught in a slammed door, headlong brought up sharp
by the ruler's snap across them. Double bars
came down like a shutter, and the last notes dangling
outside the metronome's strict iron frame
were green twigs of another music, leaves
put forth to shine elsewhere.

                              A convent yard:
raked gravel, twelve foot walls, Heaven begins
with jagged bottle-glass, and Sister Martin's
tightlaced boots tipped out through a padlocked gate.
My fingers hoard their numbness. At a keyboard
killing time, all thumbs, I stroll and tumble
through twenty bars of tangled summer, thickets
of spiked black formal hedge, before I stumble
on darkness and the ditch. O Sister Martin,
straight on your stool, with metronome and ruler
counting out the beats, green sprigs like gracenotes
flourish outside the bars. What I have kept
of time, your time (four shillings an hour), is this.

Wolf Boy

Cradled and warm, fur-warm, in the she-wolf's lair:
sky howling grey, the sweet milk of the planets
to suck; wolf-brothers tumbling, playful nip
of tooth and claw; on all fours going safe
in the she-wolf's tracks and closer to the earth.

How could he guess that days of separation
would come, when he on two feet must stand taller
and naked in the air? Feeling the itch
of warm fur at his groin, in his mouth raw words
to hurl at the grey bitch sky that turned from him.

Sweating before an iron trap whose hinges
snap at a foreleg, kneeling to sniff blood
that streaks wet meadow grass. Pricking an ear
in his attic bed for lean wolf-packs that prowl
the forest edge, their low growls in his throat.

The boots, the books, the chairs! A firelit trestle
where cream goes round, frothing in wooden cups.
The girls' bare arms disturb him. Wolf-skulls nailed
to planks and wolf-skins underfoot. The searing
blue of their entrails in the gun shot blast.

Sulking and blond. Ashamed of his footsteps printing
the snow, of water jerked from a pump that stings
like nettles on the chest, soft stroke of hands
in a game of blindman's buff. Ashamed to suffer
the strange goosepimpling of his hairless flesh.

At night past the last hut slouching, barred helm tower
with its slew black cross, a neighbour's grim face clenched
on its own, its human grief. Caught in the red
-eyed blaze of the wolf's slow agony, its shadow
on all fours, shaggy, limping at his heel.

This Day Under My Hand

for Jill and Lance Phillips

Well it was never mine,
not really. My father bought it
in my name to save
the tax in '45:
streaked weatherboard, no view
to speak of, only the sand
-hills of Moreton Island,
humpbacked and white like whales.

My sister will stock its rooms
with cedar and brass,
her kids leave sandprints of
their sneakers on its floors,
small arms spread to conjure
again from moonlit shallows
the old rock cod they hooked
at dawn out on the reef.

Sandcrabs throw their claws
in a copper pot, hiss
red, their agonies
sealed off under a lid.
At nine the Scrabble board,
small words interlocking
down and across that fill
an evening square by square.

Storm-lanterns. Tigermoths
at the wirescreen door. Slow fan
of the light at Cowan Cowan.
The cold Pacific banging—
an open gate. Australia
hitched like a watertank
to the back verandah, all night
tugging at our sleep.

8

A world away, and nothing
to do with me: shearwater
gulls, the sun-drenched crevice
where lobsters crawl, sharp salt
stinging the flesh like bees,
working its slow way into
the cracks in iron, laying
its white crust on the skin.

Now let it go, my foothold
on a continent!—I sigh
my name, it blooms elsewhere
as salt, gull's cry, bruised flesh
of the reef that gasps and thrashes
its life out in our hands.
From the dark bay hissing
like crabs, red tropic suns.

Poem

You move by contradictions:
out of a moment
of silence far off
in Poland or January
you smile and your body
returns to my touch.

Entering a winter
room I find myself
dazzled: all summer
in the throats of vases, windows
ablaze with air, our pear-tree
brimming with wasps.

My dull hands follow
at night your unseasonable
kindling and cooling
through twelve dreams and the twelve
colours of darkness
between midnight and dawn.

Birthday Poem

Keine sichtbaren Narben
keine Medaillen

At thirty: no visible scars,
no medals. Having survived
the several deaths (not all
my own) I've walked away from
and putting on flesh,
I stand at the bright sill watching
a northern town grow real
through fog. Soft green climbs into
the beeches, night hauls off.

How far? One step's enough
or the world's too small
to walk in up and down
between four walls of air.
Brightboy goes plain-sailing,
till mother's apron strings
snap. How far
do we fall? What country after
is solid to the heel?

Dawn: black rooftops lighted
by rain. Its softness
feathers their hard edge, birds
start up. Downstairs the clatter
of plates, the day's first
traffic. Life begins
with small things: water splashing
from taps, dogs sniffing
at lamp-posts and grass.

I watch the newsboy figure
-of-eight on burning wheels
and toss it in, the morning
rolled on its lies, twelve inches

of sunlight on the path.
Go down and take it up,
unfold it. The sun ticks
but does not explode. Another
day. So far, so good!

At a School Athletics Day

Strollers of April green: white tent-poles hold
the sky, the crowd's breath catches
on the heel of a javelin thrower,
a boy as thick as two short planks who never
will learn to distinguish
between perfect past and past conditional.

I walk between hurdles fallen,
on a cinder track where sprinters kneel, with two
friends, my former students, freed
from blue serge to the daring
of corduroy and sideburns,
the faded blue-sky blue of washed-out jeans.

They argue: was Prince Hamlet hesitant
of murder lest the act
define him with its blood (he being for his taste
too narrowly defined
already by the too too sullied flesh);
or was he

(long shaft steady now)
caught, rat's foot and star,
in the metaphysical mousetrap, O so subtly
baited with death,
that his timid soul, nose twitching in the darkness,
sniffed and nibbled at?

Questions indeed for a clear spring day, sun breeding
desire like daffodils,
the dead in green troughs nudging
our heels. And was he
twenty—they mean like *them*—
or balding, short of breath, a curious reader between the
lines

of documents and faces,
well-meaning, impassioned, vague, an eternal student
                                        pushing thirty,
like *me*? So time breaks
on the skull's bleak promontory, idle fellows
exit underground, and April raises
questions, or daffodils, out of their end.

On the far side of the field the crowd's breath lifts
away over our head, steel
flies to nail its shadow in the grass.
Falling, not out of sight but where
two schoolboys in sneakers
run up snow-footed with a measuring tape.

Snow

A stirring as among
cattle that lift their heads
through darkness to the scent
of water, horses snuffing

at thunder in the grass.
And nothing today will keep them
quiet or still
in the pinewood desks or summon

their eyes to reflect
figures and cold facts
from the blackboard. They brim
with light, a window-square

where trees writhe, sky glows greenish
bronze and staggers white
like surf. Their senses catch it
from far off, something moves

toward them, edging closer
even than lead pencils,
cats, chalk or the salty
creases in clothes,

an excitement whose crystals
fall through their veins,
the spaces of their skull,
wavering towards them

(animal eyes, the nostrils
flared) like the feathers
of owls, angel sky-flakes
blessing the dull cobbles

and slant black roofs, bare playground,
pond. On their hands the taste
of stars, a foreign coldness,
colour of distances

and all that is further off
than flesh. Falling light
strikes upward. Its brightness
creaks under our shoes.

Thaw

The season midnight: glass
cracks with cold. From lighted shop windows

girls half-sleeping, numb with frost step out.
We warm their hands between our hands, we kiss them

awake, and the planets
melt on their cheeks.

First touch, first tears. Behind their blue eyes darkness
shatters its pane of ice. We

step through into a forest
of sunlight, sunflowers.

Suburban

Safe behind shady carports, sleeping under
the stars of the Commonwealth and nylon gauze.

Asia is far off, its sheer white mountain-peaks, its millions
of hands. Shy bush-creatures in our headlamps

prop and swerve; small grass under the sprinklers
dreams itself ten feet tall as bull ants lumber

between its stems, but leans
toward Sunday morning and the motor blades.

Safe behind lawns and blondwood doors, in houses
of glass. No one throws stones. The moon dredges

a window square. Chrome fittings
hold back the tadpole life that swarms in dams.

But there are days
after drinks at the Marina when dull headaches

like harbour fog roll in, black cats give off
blackness, children writhe out of our grip,

and only the cottonwool in medicine bottles stands between
us
and the capsules whose cool metallic colours

lift us to the stars. Barefoot we drift
in sleep to the edge of town; pale moondust flares between
our toes,

ghosts on a rotary hoist fly in the wind.
Under cold white snowpeaks tucked to the chin we stare

at an empty shoe like Monday.
Sunlight arranges itself beyond our hands.

On Refusing an
All-risk Insurance Policy

Blue slate on the roof where pigeons
walk. Between walls
dust and the furious nightlife
of spiders. In the room
under the roof we venture
alone upon sleep.

The middle floor is open
to callers: cigar-ash
and the small surf of excitement
that froths on beer; changing
colours of conversation
rainbow the air.

Below in the light of dented
saucepans, an onion
sprouts on the sill;
dull metal and dishwater,
the sun in a knifecase,
the dolour of spoons.

All safe as houses—fire
kennelled in a matchbox,
the water of drowned valleys
dammed behind taps.
Barring accidents, or malice.
Nothing's disaster proof.

Fat tongues may lick at doorknobs
and dead fish rot
in drawers thick with mud.
These are the minor hazards
we live with, who climb
to sleep in the giant's mouth.

Bicycle

for Derek Peat

Since Thursday last the bare living-room
of my flat's been occupied
by a stranger from the streets, a light-limbed traveller.

Pine-needle-spokes, bright rims, the savage downward
curve like polished horns
of its handlebars denote

some forest deity, or deity of highway
and sky has incognito set up residence, the godhead
invoked in a machine.

To the other inmates of the room, a bookcase,
two chairs, its horizontals speak
of distance, travelling light. Only the mirror

remains unruffled, holding
its storm of light unbroken, calmly accepting
all traffic through its gaze. Appease! Appease! Even

this tall metallic insect,
this angel of two geometries
and speed. So much for mirrors. As for myself

I hardly dare look in. What should I offer
a bicycle? Absurd
to lay before its savage iridescence—

grease-drops' miraculous resin,
the misty Pleiades—
my saucer of sweat.

Now time yawns and its messengers appear.
Like huge stick insects, wingless, spoked with stars,
they wheel through the dusk towards us,

the shock wave of collision still lifting
their locks, who bear our future
sealed at their lips like urgent telegrams.

Sheer Edge

Here at the sheer edge
of a continent dry weed
clutches, grey gulls turn
from the sea and gather
here, precariously
building their nest.

And here too at the edge
of darkness where all floors
sink to abyss, the lighted
bar is of light
the furthest promontory
and exit sheer fall,

though words slide off, and hands
catching fail to hold,
here also may flower,
precarious as weed
or grey gull's nest, the moment
of touching, the poem.

Asphodel

Under this real estate—squared street on street
of split-level houses
with carport, garden swing—a chain
of waterlily ponds, arm of a sea
that has long since receded,
still sleeps under the still sleep of this suburb, showing
itself in flashes after rain.

We used to spend whole days there, skylarking
on an inch of blood-red water
we harried black marsh birds through weed-thick
                       shallows, the moon rose
heavy beneath us,
it tugged at our heels.
Now kids swing between pines, small limbs at nightfall
shine in the trees.

And once I almost drowned, stepping from clear skies
                       ankle deep
into aeons of mud. I gaped, the earth
rushed in. From the clamorous bottom of the night
I saw my life
of Now-I-lay-me-down and milk and clean sheets
                       out of reach
on the lily pond's black surface.
An angel plucked me out.

Face down in the blady grass and pummelled alive again
                       I gagged
on unfamiliar breath; my belly's
mud gave up its frogspawn; waterspouts and cataclysms
broke from my lungs. Filled
a moment with its strangeness I discovered
a lifelong taste for earth: gills flared
at my throat, plant fossils sprouted in my thumbs.

Now the pond too is drained. Petrol bowsers
mark the spot where twice I took my small life down to
touch

the kingdom of fishbones
and came up again. Lawn sprinklers turn. Station wagons
cruise under the leaves. Overhead,
through bars of moon-washed cloudwrack,
the night lights of planes.

A frog gulps on the path, earth-bubble green, deep water
speaks in its throat.
And revenant at dawn a pale fog ghosts among wrought-
iron furniture a shoal

of vanished lily ponds. I walk
on their clear light again and will not sink,
not this time. The garden
glows. Earth holds firm under my heel.

Adrift

Adrift in her Parker Knoll
rocking chair, my mother
rocks this way and that
in this room and that room
of a stranger's house—the new
two-roomed flat she calls
her unit, never home.
A unit: but of what?
Where now is the whole?

And brought from the house
at Hamilton her solid
antique furniture—
chairs, bed-ends, a credenza
stacked against the wall,
piled up without thought
for use or for order.
Haphazard: an image of
the way things never were.

My sister's kids come brawling
around her knees, bring
bits of a jigsaw puzzle
to sort in her lap:
a dazzle of sea—or is it
sky? the bricks and mortar
of somebody's house.
Her own is tenanted
by strangers; who leave the lights

ablaze in empty rooms,
bang doors, let kittens pee
on cushions, scratch at chairs.
In a corner of afternoon
gilt-edged and insecure

since my father's tough heart slammed
and shut her out, she rocks
in the late sun, a ghost
the sun does not shine through.

Confessions of an Only Child

for my Sister

Two years five days between us, and my nose
(or rather, grandfather's)
put firmly out of joint. Then half the length
of a pool over the hundred metres dash
to my masculinity. You were like father, I like mother,
a happy compromise—though we were seldom
                              on speaking terms
and scrapped like tigers mostly. I wrote you out
of my childhood, preferring
afternoons without you, a moony child practising thunder
by Czerny, Clementi,
to our closetings together through chicken pox,
                              slow wet weeks
at the beach house playing euchre for film star swaps.
My afternoons in fact
were yours. The poems are also yours, and empty
without you. Now there are deaths
between us, and a marriage, three hectic stars
you've captured from the dark. They flare, they plunge
                              away, go flying
down the wet beach. We are left
alone as in our earliest photograph: a stack of ruined
                              sandcastles
between us, behind
the last patch of scrub, grey ringbarked trunks in winter
                              sunlight; ahead
a night of carbide lamps. Like stars on brilliant claws
                              battalions
of soldier crabs death-rattle
and wheel across the zodiac, sand granules
pour through my fist. The Pacific poised
on a day late in the 'thirties rolls its thunder
towards us, pulled awry

by the moon. Our faces gather
their lines, their light, we grow like one another, the high
cheekbones
of parents and other strangers
rise under the skin. We might be twins at last, with nothing
between us, no time at all. Burned to a blackness
we smile into the sun.

Early Discoveries

I find him in the garden. Staked tomato plants are what
he walks among, the apples of paradise. He is eighty
and stoops, white-haired in baggy serge and braces. His
                                        moustache,

once warrior-fierce for quarrels in the small town of Zahle,
where honour divides houses, empties squares, droops and
                                        is thin
from stroking. He has come too far from his century to care

for more than these, the simplest ones: Webb's Wonders,
                                        salad-harmless,
stripped by the birds. He pantomimes a dervish-dance
among them and the birds creak off, his place at evening
                                        filled

by a stick that flares and swipes at air, a pinstriped waistcoat
                                        stuffed
with straw. It cuffs and swivels, I'm scared of it. Such temper-
                                        tantrums
are unpredictable; blind buffeting of storms that rattle

venetians, hiss off pavements in the sun. Grandpa is milder,
but when he hefts us high his white hairs prickle and the
                                        smell
is foreign. Is it garlic or old age? They are continents

I have not happened on, their time will come. Meanwhile he
                                        mutters
blessings, I watch him practise his odd rites, hatchet in hand
as he martyrs chickens in the woodblock's dark, an old man
                                        struggling

29

with wings, or shakes a sieve while bright grain showers in a
                                                        heap
and blown chaff flies and glitters, falling to the other mouths.
He comes and goes with daylight. He is the lord of
                                        vegetables,

the scourge of birds and nuns, those shoo-black crows his
                                        sullen daughters
taunt him with. His black-sheep son feeds rabbits live to
                                        greyhounds
in a cage behind choko-vines. The girls too go to the bad

in a foreign land, consorting with Carmelites, on hot nights
                                        tossing
on their high beds in a riot of lace doilies, painted virgins,
unwed. They dwell in another land. As I do, his eldest

grandson, aged four, where I nose through dusty beanstalks
                                        searching
for brothers under nine-week cabbages. He finds me there
and I dig behind his shadow down the rows. This is his
                                        garden,

a valley in Lebanon; you can smell the cedars on his breath
and the blood of massacres, the crescent flashing from ravines
to slice through half a family. He rolls furred sage between

thumb and stained forefinger, sniffs the snowy hills: bees
                                        shifting
gold as they forage sunlight among stones, churchbells
wading
in through pools of silence. He has never quite migrated,

the weather in his head still upside-down as out of season
snow falls from his eyes on Queensland's green, and
                                        January's
midwinter still. These swelling suns are miracles. Tomatoes

in invisible glasshouses sweat in the heat of his attention,
like islands Colombus happens on. And me, whom he also
finds
squatting, eggplant tall and puzzled by his dark hands
parting

the stems. Where am I? This is Brisbane, our backyard. We let
him
garden here behind a lattice wall. This house is ours
and home. He comes like a stranger, warrior-moustachioed,

un-Englished. These days I find him at all turns. One morning
early in Chios, I raise the shutter, and his garden,
re-discovered,
shines: cucumbers, spinach, trellised vines. The old man finds
me

watching; smiles and nods. Later, fresh on the marble step
in yesterday's newspaper (words of a tongue I cannot read)
his offering: two heads of new spring cabbage. I look under

the leaves (an ancient joke), there's nothing there. Just a
sprinkling
of black soil on the headlines of another war, shaken
from the roots. That night I eat them, boiled, with oil and
vinegar.

Evergreen

At twenty an admirer
of crocus and hyacinth, all
those dawn stars like snowflakes
lighting the grass,
I expected like them
to burn out fast, touch-paper
flaring, gone
in a quick blast before thirty.
How else should one live?

And here I am a decade
on from that early death.
Having seen
thirty and the years
beyond, it's the stolid ones, the inchling
head-in-cloud slow growers
I envy—turning
stars in their branches, holding
fast to the earth.

It's trees I look for nowadays,
year after year
adding their rings. Recording
this month's frost, that season's
burning, the arrival
and departure of leaves, birds,
mice, barefoot invaders,
and applecore wars
in the kingdom of twigs.

I've discovered an old man's folly,
I'm planting giants: wych elm,
chestnut, larch—a seed
cast into the next
long-shadowed century.

I doze in the shade
of a bunya-pine, its roots
deep in the 1880s,
bubbling with doves.

In its wind-rocked boughs the heavy
green Pacific drowses,
my grandfather sets sail
to find us—the tree
is dreaming our lives.
Its dust-thick shadow reaches
the road, and I swing
high on a tide of voices.
Green, green, evergreen.

An Ordinary Evening at Hamilton

The garden shifts indoors, the house lets fall
its lamp light, opens
windows in the earth

and the small stars of the grass, the night insects,
                                        needlepoint
a jungle more dense
than any tapestry, where Saturn burns, a snow owl's
                          nest, and melons feed

their crystal with hot sugars of the moon. The Pacific
breaks at our table,
each grain

of salt a splinter of its light at midday, deserts
flare on the lizard's tongue. Familiar rooms
glow, rise through the dark—exotic islands; this house

a strange anatomy
of parts, so many neighbours in a thicket:
hair, eyetooth, thumb.

Episode from an Early War

Sometimes, looking back, I find myself, a bookish nine
year old, still gazing down
through the wartime criss-cross shock-
proof glass of my suburban primary school. Blueflint gravel
ripples in my head, the schoolyard throbs. And all the players
of rip-shirt rough-and-tumble
wargames stop, look on in stunned surprise:
Hector, hero of Troy,
raw-bloody-boned is dragged across the scene
and pissed on and defiled,
while myrmidons of black flies crust his wounds and the
                                        angelic
blunt-faced ones, the lords of mutilation,
haul off and watch.

My way home
that Friday, like any other afternoon,
was the same familiar crossing of three streets, past a shop
                                        that sold
Nigger Chews and Bulls' eyes, the fig-tree gloom
of Musgrave Park where metho drinkers slept
in a buzz and flammable haze, their red-eyed
                flame-in-foxhole nightmare
the scraping of a match;

I knew then that the war, our war,
was real: highways of ash
where ghostly millions rise out of their shoes and go barefoot
nowhere, the children herded into vans
for their journey, or white-walled spick-and-span
                bath houses, suddenly trapped
by their craving for breath. At night, fogbound in mid-
                                        Atlantic,

my still sleep was choked
with bodies, blind kittens
in the tub where Mrs Allen did our wash
still jerked at arm's distance, kicking their life out in a sack.
Immaculate, stiff with starch
my shirts after that
creaked, their collars scratched. Our days were green,
                              matter-of-fact,
happy. Only at night
far out in the shipping-lanes
I foundered, white fog thickened in my throat.

Decade's End

Stocktaking: what have I put
away out of these seven
fat years to be used
against the seven lean?

Postcards of travel: slow
Rhine barges towing
cathedrals through fog;
towards dawn the Aegean

breaking dolphin-backed
with islands. Twice
in a cool decade love
that wrings us dry wrung me

dry. I survived
as we all did Cuba's
nine day hiss and splutter.
Like straw men caught

with a matchbox in the wind,
we kindled at a spark, we
were dry sticks and newsprint
pouring out smuts,

and I dreamed of the hornets' nest
my father burned, black
earwax dripped, the wingless
stumbling from Troy.

We burn, but so slowly
consuming our fats
that we barely feel it—candles
trembling and swaying,

feeding the body's flame
we glow, we fade, not all
of us even in seven
years can be renewed.

But the light at least is something
to read by. Till we learn
to do without it—growing
accustomed to the dark.

A Charm Against the Dumps

Shoo! be far off! fly
on owl's-wing feather-duster
be sucked into the belly
of Hoover go swirling
down plughole you

Bumbo lord of the dumps lord
of toothache and hay fever
of thumbnail by hammer
blackened spent matches
nose-bleeds razor-nicks

and all you left-handed
dialers of wrong numbers
stammerers stumblers
and tittle-tats madcap
demons at the wheel

the charm against your sullen
mischief is sneezing
at sunshine cold keys
slipped between skin and sweater
or counting to ten

but best of all Bumbo
lord of the dumps is shouting
so loud under the blankets
you tumble out ears ringing
the right side of the bed

The Little Aeneid

Set out then with all
your little household demons
stowed in a trunk
—bad habits that the natives
of Port Said or Aden
may relieve you of and Brisbane
unburned since invaders
(though you signalled to them nightly
from the mangroves) neglected
to land. Hungry for ashes,
betrayals, a clean break,
you rode your Pegasus, your Trojan horse,
down Albert Street. Alas
there was nothing in it! Night
came on, the city slept
behind iron lace verandahs,
the first trams rattled in.
Legends nowadays
are hard to get started
and the gods aren't easy
to believe in, let alone
offend. Still, there's always
time, and the bay
open between islands, a blue sky shrill
with voices, not all of them
gulls. Start today
with a poker game and push
your luck. Tomorrow
try your hand with Venus. Meanwhile laze
on the deck, let the weather
polish you to bronze, put on
la cuirasse héroïque. With the epic
two days out from land, a thousand
lines break loose, the apron
strings of a suburban
Dido snap, the new life

beckons—a coast whose every promontory
glitters with artefacts, plains
all air, by moonlight ghostly
with stick-white asphodel.
In your loins the dragon
howls for empire. Time
like a new land awaits
your entry. Give it
a name. Three syllables: say, Italy.

Among the Ruins

for Pam

A late arrival on the scene, I stood in '59
in the shadow of Titus' arch, watching pigeons
in their brief season fluff
and preen among the columns, inheriting
old nesting places high in a dung-patched cornice. There
were ruins
everywhere that year, though the war was fourteen years
behind us and the Fall
of Rome back further still. I had missed the best of it: the
Forum
empty, kraters drained of all but dust
in their mottled museum cases, goldleaf snatched
from the Pantheon restored as Bernini's screwball
Baldicchino. When
was Europe not in ruins? The long nave leads to water-meadow
where sad-eyed Jerseys kneel. In the Lady Chapel
at Ely, knocked-off fourteenth-century heads
still bear the hammer-blows, deliberate, true, of a sixteenth-
century
passion for purity—the shattered forms still beautiful,
more human, to each at this point
a broken monument. Nothing is missed. Bees take our sugars
—cherry stones in a bag, gilt flakes of Danish pastry—climb
fur-balling, sticky-feelered towards honey
mouths, a riven hive. It is the ruins behind Mantegna's
Saint Sebastian
that move us: splendid, pitiless,
dismembered, they stand
for more than the official
brutalities that stretch a saint or make a neat pincushion
of flesh. Their shadows
grow in the mind
of latecomers like us. Among such crumbs of masonry
we build our Eternal City, in time open
to Vandals, bee-swarms, death, a visiting breeze.

In the Grand Manner

To achieve at last
a tomb in the grand manner
eloquence and angels
are necessary, pure
poetry of effects. Aswirl
in the big winds that bluster down a nave Gianlorenzo's
ecstatic drapery
lacks nothing but body,
and that you will supply; with the smaller mouths
of course, let us not forget
them, engaging
piecemeal in the gloom
on their lesser projects: today
an eye, tomorrow
to be devoted to the lid, it takes time
to produce a masterpiece. Which
of your critics took such pains,
or came so close, dismantling crumb by crumb
your delicate achievement?
A lifetime's polishing! How your bones
will shine, even here
in the dark. Behind a right arm
raised as it were to bless
the multitude, new life
seethes, a mounting wave. When
did such passion, such a hunger
fill you? A million
small mouths chant
in the silence, white-cowled monks explore the full
range (O Gesualdo!)
that sounds beyond the flesh.
A mass in the grand manner
is being celebrated. Lay
your ear to marble, catch
a soughing like the wind
in hollows underground. This

is Eternity. Many
mouths will bring it to you. Not all
blow trumpets, not all
perform in the grand manner. There are occasions
when smaller mouths will do.

Bad Dreams in Vienna

for Judith

Past midnight turning east at the Deutsches Eck, a shallow
                                                    corner
where the first legions broke out of the wood. A little ice-age
settles in, like Charlemagne's iron crown its fierce grip
                                                    tightens

from Aix to the Pyrenees, Belle Ile to where the Danube
                                                    swinges
its tail to lash the Balkans. It is the shadow of empire falls
to mark the shaky boundary of dreams. Old verbs contain

the anarchist's plot, there are fingerprints all over. A
                                        province breaks
away but can't shake off the small clerk's passion for gold
                                                    braid,
gilt saints, diminished sevenths and *Schlagobers*. Nightmares
                                                    drag us

back to the same address. Sweating in snowfields of white
                                                    sheets
tonight at the Hotel Graben, a million dead turn in my sleep
as the great wheel in the Prater turns on the breath of
                                        children sleeping

at Döbling, Rudolfsheim, the Freudian suburbs. Over garden
tables of rustic wood, black ironwork angels creak, dark
                                                    exiles
gather, gunfire rattles the canal. Snowclouds come lowering

in off the Polish plain, a new invasion from the east.
Flakes drop their dark—fat ashes. In frozen pipes typhus
                                                    bacilli
wait, dreaming of heatwaves. The Turks are always at the
                                                    gate.

Blind hands poke over scrap heaps in the wind: a begging
                                                      letter
of Mozart, the slum where Hitler mooned, worn shaving
                                              brushes, gold
-rimmed spectacles, gold fillings, the foul breath of a
                              death's-head party

whistling *Wiener Blut*. I wake towards morning and look out
on the snowbound square, the Graben, grave or ditch. The
                                          great Pestäule
a column of white worms writhes out of its pit, and touched
                                              by winter

light the long dead wrestle, wave upon wave, hard heel on
                                              shoulder
surge upward, choke for breath. The survivor's warm breath
                                        freezes. Here
bad dreams have monuments. Their agents yawn and lick
                              the moon.

Report from Champagne Country

Such green–gold days: old vines knot in the sun, and Pol de
Limbourg's
Tres Riches Heures unwind their gothic tendrils. The vinestock
knows
what's here. Black-pudding land, the sluice where an artery
was drained,

a whole generation in the field, two armies deadlocked
still. They push an inch this way that way as earth resettles
under them, and silence; shinbone, brain-pan, clavicle

parting in the shambles. A cartwheel splinters; crossbow,
rifle
move off from the hand; the wars go on. From random shots
in May 1940 through richer strata, chivalry

and tribal skirmishes in woods ploughed under. Chantry
chapels
ride over their bones, the land is thick with minerals,
an intelligence still active as chins tilt skyward, lower ranks

spring to the alert. Dispersed in wheatfields, a platoon
spreads out, trailing as old-man's-beard from fenceposts,
early runners
of the green revolution. I've an uncle under here;

another uncle coughed all through my childhood the
corrosive
airs of La Belle France, its gold light tickled in his chest.
Good years and heady for some, the bubbling 'twenties.
He choked at last

on his bawdy anecdotes, went back to the regiment; another
gold-leaf hero sunk in the minds of boys pissed off with
honour
-boards and manhood's rare, impulsive gift. I come to judge

for myself. Hell's under here. I stoop and scrabble at the
earth.
Our century is topsoil inches thick, a cover of herbage,
and suddenly I'm there: mess tins, webbing, a howitzer-
shell

hard-packed with char and powdery red dust, the heat of
battle
cooling. Metal burns to slow extinction. Not to be softened
yet or for decades yet, or gathered back. Launching free

of its course round the earth's true magnet, it becomes mere
space-trash, debris
of a happening not of its own dimension, war economies
unloading here their surplus, thirty million factory-hands,

grey ghostly legions clubbed with sleep, sleepwalking.
Ground-fog rolls
towards them. At trench-rat level on their bellies or
balanced over
a quagmire of bones, they dream their lifetime on the
duckboards

in the jobless years, the dole and bread-queue cities, lose
their nerve
and slip. Regulation boots, belt, helmet, tins of bully take
them
down with the other faces. They sink through battles,
weeks of mud

to a green place out of war. At ease and easy, big hands
loosen,
fill with earth. Under autumn's oak-leaf cluster, out of range
of field-glass scrutiny, they shift to a softer focus, growing

used to such neighbours now as snail-shell fossils, woodlice,
                                                          tongues
that lick their brows for salt. They make their separate
                                              peace: for this one
warm rain and nettle soup, for that one shell shock, a steel
                                                          splinter

that climbs six feet to settle in the brain; and death that
                                                          faltered
once in no-man's-land surprises them in the no-man's-land
of suburban Sunday morning; they find their slow way back
                                                          to earth.

It is quiet now, out here. Though the mind wears thin at this
                                                      point, even
at midday; cattle stare into dead men's eyes, slow jaws mull
                                                          over
enigmas, energies at work down there, brutal illusions

we are not done with yet, the good years go on happening.
Two uncles lost, no firm ground won on either side. The
                                                          iron
hedges sprout new barbs and will not be grubbed out in my
                                                          lifetime,

the peace is illusory. From the earth dark bubbles climb,
                                                          invade
the bloodstream, burst and flood our consciousness.
                                  There are manoeuvres
in all these fields. And a mustering in streets of the old
                                              divisions,

the flash of savage creeds, a longing—wilful, absolute—
to be finished with all this, a passion for certitude, to enter
the pure state of the Future, unique and terrible citizenship

for which nothing, not flesh, not blood, is pure enough, and
                                        the earth too deeply
stained with humanity to be our place of resurrection.
And still the dead climb back. From battlefields, ghettos of
                                                            ash

in the blacksoil lands the *Untermenschen* stir, all energy
in a free state finding eyes in tubers, limbs in pale birch
                                                    saplings.
The plump fruit swells to bursting-point. An excitement not
                                                    our own

too long held back, bursts through us, green–gold summers
                                        on a time-fuse
exploding in our flesh. In the glare and oven-heat of
                                        wheatfields
grain crowds towards a fence, the cry of more than insects
                                                    wavers,

ascendant on the breeze. Their lives, our lives too deeply
                                                    mingled
to speak with a voice that is not theirs, who find in
                                        our drunken shambling
the first steps of a dance. At the threshing even dust is gold.

A Poet Among Others

A poet, after all, is just a human being like any other and he is bound to end up in the most ordinary way, in the way most typical for his age and his times, meeting the fate that lies in wait for everyone else.

Nadezhda Mandelstam

The self is like smoke
drifting up at dawn, a fist
can't hold it, a knotted handkerchief.

It fades into grey
winter skies. It goes where the birds go when water cracks
in pools and is no window.

Grey faces, grey serge uniforms in the frozen yard, a rollcall
                                        without
names. Midday strikes
clean through these ghosts, no longer citizens, these
                                        shadows

herded behind a winter palisade they cannot pass through
to swollen fields, to thresholds
they cross only in dreams, at first light hunted from
                        Petersburg.

They have fallen out of favour—
it's a long way down. And the state is everywhere. In a
                                man's guts
it aches, in the ear of corn it shouts its slogans, in a thick
                                skull lodges

its birdsongs like lead. The way to freedom
is thin smoke ascending, a road that winds out of the hands.
Unseen it goes on

to mud-street villages where small pigs snore under a
                                            hedge.
Birds perched on the wire
go there; fly

in, light on your wrist with a scent of pinewood, can be cast
                                            into the air
and over the stockade out. Even the grass
is innocent, goes on

growing beyond a wall. In such a century the grass
is fortunate. The state
cares only for men.

This one was a poet, holding
to the is-ness of things: a blade of rye, a moment spiralling
up from the stubble field on a lark's wing

to enter the whole day's blue, a waterdrop filled with the
                                            light of Causasus,
a woman's face
clenched on its grief.

He shares it now,
the commonness of what is human: grey, grey as the dirt
with its many grains, each one identical

and singing. The earth
in his mouth at last. Heavy as silence where the unkillable
                                            grass-seed
takes root under his tongue.

At Ravenna

We are all of us exiles of one place
or another—even those
who never leave home. Umbrella pines

gather towards dusk
a darkness even the waters are not deep enough to hold.
At dawn a million needles

blaze, angels of light dance on their points, the smallest
                                        stone-chips
glint, show their colours
to rival Paradise; the long-faced poet

and failed politico, by the phantoms
of tribal warfare haunted, lordly thugs and mercenaries
dogging his heels,

dreams of a lost city, its mud still grey upon his shoes.
Arriving here
in 1959, I met on the road two miles from Forli

one of the bright new Europeans, a Belgian from Verviers—
lit up in that glorious summer with a passionate conviction
all Europe could be saved, one

continent, one people undivided. Cornstalks
sighed and the wind was in them, dark hands rattled
                                        at the husks.
We slept in a bombed-out farmhouse. All night

on the highway lorries rumbled, gothic hordes, the sky
                                        was filled
with a crying among stones as of an empire
collapsing in the wind. We woke at dawn to find its brilliant
                                        monuments

intact among shabby cafes
and factories, the dust of another town.
On Sunday, starting early from the tomb

of the last blue-eyed freebooter, through one deserted
baptistery
and the next, he talked
of Law and History and second chances, second

breaths. Three years later
from Conrad's heart of darkness: 'My students here believe
in nothing
but refrigerators dropping from the clouds

on parachutes' . . . Another pilgrim seeking
to wipe out the stain—
finding at last its shadow was his own. Out of a cloudless

sky over Stanleyville
the parachutes descend, spore of a sinister black pinewood
unfurling on the wind. We all die

under alien skies at a place called Ravenna. Whether the
new atlas calls it
that, or Sydney,
or Katsangani formerly Stanleyville.

Notes on an Undiscovered Continent

Hot island drifting south, over the edge of nightmares Ultra
Mare and lost. Only cyclones stumble on its reef.

Its exiles go their own way, lying low in jungle pockets
and sleepy salt backwaters, growing sideways from their
kin.

Silence: so absolute it fills the mind with a slow-worm's
giddy
horror of distances. Our counterweight to the Himalayas

and the abbeys of Normandy, Joachim's fiddle-bow, Young
Werther's
sorrows, the golden stirrups of Tamburlaine. Flat sand-
dunes ripple,

the air's alive with wings, but uncongenial to visions
or saintly levitation. Intending Josephs of Copertino

are brought down with a bump, the soul is pushed to
extremities.
The earth yields nothing to us, only wheatcrops, minerals,

no pagoda of human skulls to cast a minatory shadow,
no heroes shaking plumes of asphodel, twelve-tiered cities

in the dark of sorghum paddocks; not even the femur of a
cat.
Only high in a limestone wall the eyelid-clink of fossils
stranded

far from the sea, small lives that time sucked out. Voices also
depart, leaving no footprint; centuries powder at a touch.

The rest—since nothing happens—we must invent.
                                        As conceive
a depression off Lord Howe Island bringing migraines to the
                                        table

-lands, falling as snow on Perisher. As item: local
lore. In the summer months that end with *r* do not take
                                        crabs

from the Bay. Their sweet flesh foxes then, in mangrove
                                        thickets feeding
on sewage under the moon, they drowse and sicken. Having
                                        failed

once, the invaders turn and swarm ashore on lonely beach-
                                        heads in our dreams.
At the centre of our lives a big stone shines, we find a name

for it, perhaps our own, settle the landslip with our bones.
Such settlements are provisional. The nineteen tongues of
                                        Europe

migrate to fill a silence, we're settling in for the long wait.
And graves are a fair beginning: on fat soles now and whiter
                                        than worms

the pilgrims with their bawdy tales appear. Wild, wild
from the dead mouth a good omen, follow their wings, a
                                        crazy flight

over flowerheads. Find a new land to be tasted, map it ridge
by ridge where the dark swarms gather and refine its
                                        pollens—this

too is industry. Across the plain columns of light
are stacked, set out between them. They are the Pillars of
                                        Hercules.

Reading Horace Outside Sydney, 1970

The distance is deceptive: Sydney glitters invisible
in its holocaust of air, just thirty miles away, in Rome
two thousand years from here, a goosequill scrapes, two
                                        crack divisions
are hurled against a furclad, barbarous northern people
                                        pushing

south into history; small throats are cut at committee tables,
a marriage dies in bed; bald officials like old pennies
worn smooth by time and trade were once my copper-keen
                                        schoolfellows,
who studied Cicero and shook their heads over the fall

of virtue in high places; now on pills twelve storeys high
in air, they shake their heads and fall and pause and walk
                                        again.
Somewhere across a border shabby barefoot warriors
stumble into grass, an empire mourns, in small wars seeking

safe boundaries against death. Over the traffic, over the
                                        harbour, lions
roar, schoolboys scramble out of nightmares, mineral stocks
fall with a noiseless crash, the sigh of millions; cicadas
are heard, shrill under stones, in the long suspension of our
                                        breath.

Out here wheat breathes and surges, poplars flare. On the
                                        highway lorries
throb towards city squares. High in the blue a Cessna bi-
                                        plane
crop-dusting lucerne turns to catch the sun. The brilliant
                                        granule
climbs on out of sight. Its shadow dances in my palm.

Stooping to Drink

Smelling the sweet grass
of distant hills, too steep
to climb, too far to see
in this handful of water
scooped from the river dam.

Touching the sky where like
a single wing my hand
dips through clouds. Tasting
the shadow of basket-willows,
the colour of ferns.

A perch, spoon-coloured, climbs
where the moon sank, trailing
bubbles of white,
and schoolkids on picnics
swing from a rope—head

over sunlit heels like angels
they plunge into the sun
at midday, into silence
of pinewoods hanging over
a sunken hill-farm.

Taking all this in
at the lips, holding it
in the cup of my hand.
And further down the hiss
of volcanoes, rockfall

and hot metals cooling
in blue–black depths a hundred
centuries back.
Taking all this in
as the water takes it: sky

sunlight, sweet grass-flavours
and the long-held breath
of children—landscape
mirrored, held a moment,
and let go again

Off the Map

All night headlamps dazzle
the leaves. Truck drivers
throbbing on pills
climb out of the sleep

of farm towns prim
behind moonlit lace, bronze Anzacs
dozing, leaden-headed,
at ease between wars,

and out into a dream
of apple orchards, paddocks
tumbling with mice,
bridges that slog the air,

black piers, bright water, silos
moonstruck, pointing nowhere
like saints practising stillness
in a ripple of grain.

They thunder across country
like the daredevil boys
of the 'fifties who flourished
a pistol in banks,

and rode off into headlines
and hills or into legends
that hang, grey-ghostly, over
campfires in the rain.

Now kids, barefooted, wade
in the warm, hatched tyre-marks
of country dust, the print
of monsters; cattle stare.

All night through the upland
spaces of our skull
in low gear shifting skyward
they climb towards dawn.

A lit butt glows, a beer can
clatters. Strung out
on the hills, new streets that shine
in the eyes of farmboys, cities

alive only at nightfall
that span a continent.
Nameless. Not to be found
by day on any map.

Pieces for a Northern Winter

I

The steps by which winter
comes to us, moving
down through a scale

to the low note of the owl, a booming
in snowfields that narrow
their focus to blue.

The last days of November
smoking. A streetlamp
discovers Muscovy,

a bear's white polar shadow
sheets the river's breath.
Each day now has the sharpness

of a tooth and December
shines under our clothes. Moving
fast across the snow

towards us, the new year
leaves no print. We're lost. The rescue-party
will not find us now.

II

Fine scribble-lines of ice: the lake tenses
its skin, gives up

its wings. Wave upon wave, snow-capped they flow
south into the sun, birches shudder

and give up their leaves.
Austerities—a tightening. Of belts as horizons

crackle and shrink. The smallest whisper
travels in nine-league boots,

a giant
snores in the mouse's ear,

and salted, frozen on hooks, the autumn
kill shakes off

its thunder of hooves. On metal plates
the small bones, creaking,

nudge at distances. Spring
already and the awakening! We eat

with a slow solemnity. Resurrection
is real and will take place in every fashion: sucked

of their marrow even wishbones
expect it. Outside

the pack ice buckles. Listen. New leaves
can be heard breaking through

in the stillness. Hear also, in the scavenger waste-places,
the shifting of bones.

The Gift, Another Life

for Derek and Jenny Peat

The day's heat dwindles. Having shared
our few late-summer crumbs, the birds
depart. Across the valley shadows
   straggle in like herds
of slow sad cattle, hills away
a tin roof flickers out. Familiar
farmhouse stars, a silo plunging
   moonward among clouds.

I drowse between pencil pines, the stars
rise through me as in sleep I climb
in the warmth of other arms to meet
   myself. Horizons stream
away, all fences down, all frontiers
open. I am free to cross
five oceans even. At dusk these broken
   hills break free of time

and place, four generations pass
where wheel-tracks dent a slope. We share
our lives with ghosts, the future strikes
   clear through us, we are here
and gone where crumbling paddocks dream
their first green world ploughed under: feather,
fur, beaked skull, old bush ways opening
   upwards into air.

I think of friends on this side of
our star who move alone through sleep
or soar in each other's arms, and you
   out there where planets dip
low on the western rim approaching
daybreak now—snow patches struck
to pools of crocus, swallows that bring
   the first heat from the Cape.

Sunlight or shade the same day holds
us all, our cool green island floats
through space. Soiled, sullied, plundered, we
    go with it, at our wits'
end, and world's end maybe, pushing
out to the edge of night. Soon
with what dignity we've kept, and two
    by two, our dying planet's

last wild creatures, we and all
our household will set out, with stones
to touch or smell for luck, flag-iris,
    garlic, grains, a Rubens'
landscape—quitting a star we dare
not visit save in dreams, a sacred
garden closed to us; fogbound,
    radiant with bones.

But time is time enough. Though all
we do betrays us, earth, dull earth,
still tugs and beckons; pausing from work
    its greenness takes our breath.
Field upon field we stride waist high
through voices, the ground is sown with more
than mind can fathom, Love remains
    a power to be reckoned with.

And weddings are huge doors open wide
to more than sky or earth: the threshold
shines, the guests arrive—a keg
    spiked and carpets rolled
away for dancing; shy beasts stand
witness when later in the dark
a small voice claims of lovers all
    they have, a life, a world.

Violence abroad: owls dragged towards
a killing, the dominance of blood.
Sky-bullies roar and swagger. Streets

of fire and cities mad
with a yeasty turbulence as fine jaws
gnash like millstones. Cattle breathe
among boughs and feed on moonlight. Murder,
   mischief, plenitude.

Low night-sounds in the grass, another
order. I watch the new moon steer
west over rooftops, wade through dams,
   below me cities flare
as pane on pane their towers catch
the sun; its morning light will touch
all sleepers and among them you,
   on your side of our star.

Wake softly now. Steep fiords swell,
weirs drain their starlight, thin stalks push
through mud, the night sky tilts and all
   its constellations rush
before us, bare cold worlds we shall
inhabit when our world snuffs out.
But later. Light-years away their lavas
   glow, their deserts flash.

Wake easy. Now the sun comes round
to your side, brimming light expands
over gulf and delta, sickle-shaped
   it sweeps the flat wheatlands,
picks out the Alps, then leaf by leaf
chill London parks, squares, bridges, docks.
Earth turns. I turn toward sleep and pass
   the day into your hands.

To be Written in Another Tongue

As for example, the language in which my grandfather
dreams now he is dead, or living,
muttered in his sleep. Clouds

flow to a different breath, daylight moons hatch from the
                                                    stillness
of a different dark,
where owls drop from the sun, dirt-coloured starlings

by other names than we know them gather
the dusk, grain by grain let fall the shadow of their bodies.
Such ordinary events

are poems in another tongue and no translation
possible. Owl
with its heavy blood and vowel an open mouth

too slow to snatch the heads off
dustmotes. Humming-birds
like Giotto's tear-stained kamikaze angels

sorrow, having learned
their name in a dead language
is entrée to a steel-meshed aviary or Table of Contents.

some grey *Jardin des Plantes*. Grandfather mumbles
our names in the earth. We come
to light out of his mouth, oracular bubbles.

I range through the thesaurus
for a word: homesickness, yearning
of grandsons for a language

the dead still speak, the dying in their sleep still
mutter, the advent
of common objects, strange upon the tongue.

Escape from the City of Glass

A city of too much glass; too many walls
to walk through toward weekday rituals

and clouds, slow island peaks at snail's pace crossing
a pane, leaving no smudge of breath and missing,

as they slide through picture frames into ideal landscapes,
their shadow on backyard swimming pools like harps

unstrung, jangled with sunlight, sick for the boom
of surf. An exile's city much like home:

where ocean and air perfect each other, I see
too easily through my friends, and eternity

is a trick of time, of still days poised like mirrors
to catch more blue than sky or harbour wears.

Imagine, a life elsewhere! All week it snows
in my head, my thumbjoints crack. On Sunday lilos

bob in thirty degrees of sweat; a blast
of pure light strips our limbs. Later we taste

their salt where ice-sheets burn, pineforests heap
the Alps on a counterpane, the sun beats up

gold under midnight skin. After celery-sticks
and owls, the incantations. Change the locks,

escape down five dream-ladders, miraculous exit
to a city with the cool passionate climate

of the high Köchel numbers, and citizens
likewise, moving at ease in opposite zones

of the possible through un-Euclidean squares,
all circles. Above their traffic one saint gestures

skyward to where a fleet of dirigibles,
fat angels, bump and flare; another to tables

on the shady side, where strangers keep appointments,
beggars get high on change, whiffs of incense

from Borromini altars drift in clouds
about us, and heaven in all its attitudes

from thunderhead to cirrus finds reflection
in gravel ponds and stares, each face a scene

from the plain soul's need to surprise itself, each actor
a suburb—elegant, shabby, gay, austere

or whatever; as if the cast of a Monteverdi
opera (one half gods) broke into a gaudy

ensemble of Meyerbeer and found *bel canto*
their *lingua franca*. We join them: *one, two*

four—the music swerves, summer unrolls
its nature strips like carpets, seesaws, sundials,

perspective pines, an avenue all air
and blue silk finding wings, plus the formal error

whose ill-drawn stitch will save us, since no man makes
it flawless, poem or city. Even Socratics

leave something unasked, a false step where the god
may shine, and lovers who sink down in a wood

dishevelled, lost, from the night's misunderstandings
rise to find provisional happy endings

in perfect rhymes and vows sworn fathoms deep,
the promises imperfect lives must keep.

A Commentary on Galatians

Ants
file out of their holes, bearing the fragments of yesterday's
light in their bellies,
the nest a necropolis
still crowded under the hot squares of an autumn afternoon
at Cerveteri and organised
like this: grain eaters, police spies, herders
of underlings, a little Soviet
aswarm under our shoes, making for crumbs of Marie
                                        Antoinette

or Cassie's rainbow cake,
as small in the perspective
of time, at work on the pyramids,
they die in yeasty grey–black
tides round the legs
of our Early Kooka. I watch them on my belly
in the grass. They carry the sun away, sharing
its grains of fire between them
—a new Diaspora, bearing the five books and the seed
                                        of the Redeemer

piecemeal to be buried
at dusk under our lawn. There in the suburbs
under us it shines
at midnight: the godhead
fallen from our hands to be divided among the humble,
its sweetness in their mouths.

The Fables

To interpret the wood you first must fall
asleep in it, feel
its breathing lift your ribs, turn
owls out of a pocket
of fog, rub fur
in your groin and sense the hardening
of fingernails, of toenails
to horn. After that
communication's easy. You may eavesdrop on the follies of
                                                    citizens
of the other kingdom, preach
to birds. And when the fabulist
comes home, sleepwalking
the streets of a town
where his father flourished in the butcher's act, he will
                                                    suffer
them all, the solemn beasts—ox, magpie, lion,
and mad March hare; slipping
away at dusk to tame his small wolf brothers
with fables, teaching them
to know—dreaming buckets
of thick sow's blood—themselves transformed, turned
                                skin-side out, forgiven
the crimes they move to in their guise as men.

Metamorphoses

The forbidden name: spelled out on a screen as wheatgrain
flicker, scribbled on pavements, the initials
that blood makes trailed from knives. A blond grease-
                                        monkey
slides out under axle-bars and wears the Smile,

a deus ex machina. The Word at this point
enters someone's head, a stutter finding
speech in the slow vernacular of locals.
An eye among rosebuds winks from an open fly

and half a county quickens, so many siblings,
tongue-tied, snub-nosed, tufted, gravely conceiving
of father as a hepped-up Maserati.
A buzz some schoolboy swats is left for spiders

to drag out of the sun: announcing OM,
his name, too low to cut through conversations.
No words pass between species. Nothing changes.
This angle of light the gospels will get wrong.

The Elements of Geometry

In this bankers' town, of course art would depend
on figures, angles, rules
of thumb. The shadow of the Palazzo Vecchio
shifts across the air, a slow diagonal, cutting
violets with its edge
of ice, an imaginary
triangle of which
my clenched fist is the base and Judith's upraised cleaver one
point, the Banca Toscana perhaps another,
or the sun that holds in focus
a province and its skulls. How curious, Dante, that our lines
of life should intersect
in this narrow street, you going
your way to the exile's tomb, I seeking
mine. (This line of thought extended downward
would pass through New Zealand
and upwards might divide
the Fathers of the Church in holy schism.) Spaces gather
in the evening light—huge, solemn, empty, howling
for blue, to be occupied with small events
from the passion of a saint or miracles
in the repertoire of God. What feeling is it for the structure
of things, another law,
that makes this old man pause at the mathematical
centre of the Square? These are other kingdoms
than nature. This city
is the capital of more than Tuscany. All lines meet here
                    The bright cube opens,
turns and splits in segments. We enter
at a tangent to the field, our only asset
an eye and its mechanics, the ground rules of a discipline.

Guide to the Perplexed

As unpredictable as picnic weather, blue
eyes shine from the heads of perfect bullies,
angels turn away, the Golden Casket's drawn, for no
good reason a terminal illness is arrested. This
too a sort of gift—to be dealt thirteen
trumps, a full hand of masterpieces. Oil fields
sleep for centuries under the camel
kingdoms. Horses are bred that carry algebra
north to solve the dreams of planet-watchers. Iron
weapons in the right hand, and a syntax
equal to the decisions that must be taken,
means more and faster highways, bigger
battles, further provinces to rule,
a land the delta floods and seed that makes
us more aggressive forebears. There is Justice
too of course; and solemnly we work
towards it. But luck comes undeserved as this world's
free and final grace. Though someone somewhere always
pays, we praise it, wishing at each season,
our friends, in life, in love, the lucky break.

Gray's Anatomy

Thumb

When did he join us,
come in out of the dark?
a pig's snout that had lost
its sense of smell—dwarf, bully, politico,
a new intelligence
with the trick of hanging on.

Latecomer of five
agents recruited
to betray us, it's the thumb, the thick, the blunt one,
                                       Machiavel,
that draws them to a fist.
Points nowhere
but down and tickles no one,
but is wondrous necessary for all business
with knives, for flicking over
banknotes and to steady
a pen.
       The others
retain a memory
of softer rituals. Having the rare power to gentle
all beasts, however savage,

save only

                  thumbs.

Appendix

Remote as Neptune's second moon, the shape
of South Vietnam and raging;
a little umbilicus

that tethers us still
to a lost continent whose creatures settle
their sharp claws in us. Neighbours,

heart and head, regard it
darkly. A disorderly republic,
it stinks and is consumed. Sleeping partners

go their own way, eye
involved with its perspectives, stomach dealing
with the fruits of the earth.

It dreams of a different body
that did not emerge, wormlike
puffs on its other island. Pickled soul or guardian angel,

it shrivels, out of use. When we cut it
out the other organs do not suffer.
The left side marks its absence with a scar.

Eyetooth

Lodged firmly in my jaw a little tombstone. Tethered once
to a doorknob, its milky predecessor
was pulled, set in a glass to focus moonlight, then buried
with elk-horn, mammoth-tusk,
in the dark under a shed.

Something of that unlucky episode
survives. Whenever
a door slams in my head
the eyetooth stirs, goes underground, consorting
with Tamburlaines and other heavier bones.

A little Mount Hopeless, listening-post for dispatches
from a mouth that opens
out there to swallow us, an eye
for seeing in the earth; from its old forays finding the thread
we hang by—the tracker
smelling out a death.

Wild Lemons

for Don Dunstan

Through all those years keeping the present
open to the light of just this moment:
that was the path we found, you might call it
a promise, that starting out among blazed trunks
the track would not lead nowhere, that being set
down here among wild lemons, our bodies were
expected at an occasion up ahead
that would not take place without us. One
proof was the tough-skinned fruit among
their thorns; someone had been there before us
and planted these, their sunlight to be sliced
for drinks (they had adapted
in their own way and to other ends); another
was the warmth of our island, sitting still
in its bay, at midnight humming
and rising to its own concerns, but back,
heat-struck, lapped by clean ocean waters
at dawn. The present is always
with us, always open. Though to what, out there
in the dark we are making for as seven o'clock
strikes, the gin goes down and starlings
gather, who can tell? Compacts made
of silence, as a flute tempts out a few
reluctant stars to walk over the water. I lie down
in different weather now though the same body,
which is where that rough track led. Our sleep
is continuous with the dark, or that portion of it
that is this day's night; the body
tags along as promised to see what goes.
What goes is time, and clouds melting into
tomorrow on our breath, a scent of lemons
run wild in another country, but smelling always of
                                        themselves.

Elegy: the Absences

G.M., 1896–1964

Tree crickets tap tap tap. They are tunnelling
their way out of the dark; when they break through,
their dry husks will be planets. Little sheep-bells
clink. The sheep are finding their way down
through clouds, and fence by fence into the distance
dogs bark, clearing ditches, marking farms.
Much that is living here goes into the mouth
of night or issues from it. I sleep, and silence
climbs into my ear, the land blacks out, all
that was delicate and sharp subdued with fog.
The dead are buried in us. We dream them
as they dreamed us and woke and found us
flesh. Their bones rise through us. These are your eyes:
you will see a new world through them. This is your tongue
speaking. These are your hands, even in sleep
alert like animals. Stumbling on
down known paths through blackberry canes I happen
on details that insist. They scratch, they drag
their small hooks, they whiplash, they draw blood.

• • •

You balloon above me, a big cloud burning
with breath; a coolness settles on my skin.
Your hands that could manage
things gone wrong, stopped clocks, a generator
with the devil in it, roughly set me right.

You talk, you stroke my brow, I come back into
the house: clean plates on shelves, the simple view
—a world that's workable.
I'm safe, I'm held. As when you found a greenie's
thin-shelled, sky-pale egg and brought it to me. Look,

You said. I looked. In the round nest of your hand
a landscape, water, stories, even my own
small life. In your palm,
roughened from work, a cat's cradle of lines,
leading to where I was, to where I am.

                    •   •   •

In a century when it was some men's fate to be
marshalled into firing squads, and others'
to go to the wall (the meat-eating

angels of those years snapped through the air
like bullets and left wounds that peace could not
grow over; even those like you who lived

at peace, had also bled); in a century
when wheatcrops passed three times through the same
                                        belly
as mud, as mud, a man walked out

of a tale you told and stood knee deep in ashes
on the moon. Your days so common I can find
no mark of 'history'. But I see you rub

a sore place on your skull, wondering where
it struck, what day, what hour, and how
you picked up the beginnings of a story we

are seeing, no not the end but say the climax
of. The man goes on out of your mouth and into
silence, hangs on a breath. What happens next?

                    •   •   •

You bore my image long enough, the promise
of it, looking clean through the bodies
of women to where I stood beside the river
waiting, pitching stones. No wonder I stand there

still. No wonder I bear the image of you
to the edge of streams in every weather, looking
back through the bodies
of women, strangers, searching for the one
door I must come through. I look back
through it, beyond the wars: a regatta day;
grass, white lace verandahs. You are there. You are looking
towards me. The woman is still, turning neither
your way nor mine, she does not know us.
She will.
    The river is always the same river.
Stones skip light across it. Generations
of fish, wave upon wave, shoulder upstream.

• • •

You knew about absences. I am learning
slowly how much space they occupy
in any house I move to, any page—the white spaces
no ink flows into, the black ones
no breath flows out of, mouths. My mother lived
for eight years in your absence. Now we make room
for hers. The ghostly bodies we grew out of
are still somewhere within us. We look through them
to what lies ahead. Back behind
is greener than it was for all those deaths.

• • •

The house catches its breath. I go downstairs
in the dark: stars at the window, a tap drips
cold. I stoop and drink from a cupped hand,
cradling the sweet water. It is more
than water when I lift it to my lips.

A barefoot child on the cool boards of a house
I left decades ago, I pause and hear
your footfall on the landing. *Is that you
son*? I dare not answer. If I went and stood
in the dark well looking up, would you be there?

First Things Last

I

The room on all sides viewless.
As if breathed on
glass, your cries
appear, ice crystals click.
A dense fog seeps in.
These are the fittings
of a clean, fluorescent, flat, unhappy country.

Its walls are soft. They melt
through you. Lift an arm
and weightless it drifts off. Other
parts of your body
are off elsewhere. You walk out over
(Careful, don't cut yourself—
that dream is red) soft breakers tipped with glass.

Only the instruments
are keen with a view
to business. They are unpacked
from a black bag, animal; the hands that use them
are also animal, and interested. Hot for blood
they start over the dazzling
absolute ice towards you, bringing night.

II

Behind you in the glass
a slow hand effaces
the room, wipes out
lake mist and forest.
Your smile

fades over the sill.
When the mirror
clears, no one stands

in the wet field that peals from
its surface. You stare

and stare. It takes days
of accounting for each hair
on your head, each grain of dust,
to imagine yourself
back into the frame.

You argue with the sky
in your mouth; you breathe out
clouds, get them moving
behind you, they lift
the grass, a little nightwind

arrives at your skin.
Slowly you manage
your head into the room. If you
can glue a face back on it,
you win.

III

We've all been in there: how
we got out, what passed, how long
we stayed is a black hole

or many in the fabric,
amnesias and pits we tumble into, deep
as first breath or the long drop where we missed

a step that was not there. Whole stars are swallowed
at a gulp. They shine
as velvet intermissions,

holes with a history. Those who come back
don't know that they have been there and have nothing
to tell. Such open

occasions in the net
are the shadow of spilt milk, black, that spirals upward, the
                                                    angel's
preliminary sneeze sucked inside out.

IV

Laying the small bones out
in rows for the moon
to suck. We call this *Living
from One Day to the Next.*

To lie tight-wrapped in butcher's
paper and bleed
events: you all know this one:
it's *Learning from History.*

You mount a bicycle
without wheels. What falls away
as you pedal uphill?
The Joys of the Flesh

The styles are as many as
the players. Strict rules
apply but can be broken.
Nobody wins.

The Crab Feast

I

There is no getting closer
than this. My tongue slips into
the furthest, sweetest corner
of you. I know all

now all your secrets.
When the shell
cracked there was nothing
between us. I taste moonlight

transformed into flesh
and the gas bubbles rising
off sewage. I go down
under mangrove roots and berries, under the moon's

ashes; it is cool
down there. I always knew that there was more
to the Bay than its glitters,
knew if you existed

I could also
enter it; I'd caught so deeply all
your habits, knowing the ways
we differ I'd come to think we must be one.

I took you
to me. Prepared
a new habitat under the coral
reef of my ribs. You hang there, broken like the sun.

II

Noon that blinding glass did not reveal us
as we were. It cast up variant selves
more real than
reflections, forms

with a life of their own,
stalk eye a periscope
that determined horizons, Doulton claws
that could snap off a thumb.

I liked that. Hence the deep afternoons
with pole and net, the deeper
nights when I went down after the tropic
sun. Hence too the Latin

names, a dangerous clawhold. I wanted the whole of you,
                                                raw poundage
in defiance of breathlessness
or the power of verbal charms,
on my palm, on my tongue

III

This the Place. I come back
nightly to find it
—still, sleepy, sunlit, presided over

by old-timers, waterbirds whose one
thin leg props up clouds,
the ruck of open water

ahead, and the hours
of deepening blue on blue the land wades into afternoon.
These then the perspectives:

matchwood pier, a brackish estuary
that flows on into
the sun, a rip of light over the dunes.

I enter. It is all
around me, the wash
of air, clear-spirit country. It goes on

all day like this. The tide
hovers and withdraws. Under the sun, under the moon's
cross-currents, shadows

fall into place
and are gathered to the dark. This hunt
is ritual, all the parties to it lost. Even the breaths

we draw between cries
are fixed terms in what is celebrated,
the spaces in a net.

Among mangrove trunks the fire-
flies like small hot love-crazed
planets switch on,

switch off. They too
have caught something. A chunk of solid midnight
thrashes in the star-knots of their mesh.

IV

You scared me with your stillness and I scared
myself. Knowing
that everything, even the footsoles of the dead, where your
                                    small mouths

nudged them, would feed

the airy process of it.
The back of my head
was open to the dream
dark your body moves in. I hunted you

like a favourite colour,
indigo, to learn

86

how changeable we are, what rainbows
we harbour within us

and how I should die, cast wheezing into
a cauldron of fog.
That was the plan:
to push on through

the spectrum to that perfect
primary death colour, out
into silence and a landscape
of endings, with the brute sky pumping red.

V

I watch at a distance
of centuries, in the morning
light of another planet
or the earliest gloom

of this one, your backward
submarine retreat,
as hoovering across
the seabed—courtly,

elate, iron-plated—
you practise the Dance
I watch and am shut out.
The terrible privacies!

You move slow motion sideways,
an unsteady astronaut:
step and counter
step, then the clash,

soundless, of tank engagement;
you might be angels
in the only condition
our senses reach them in. I observe

your weightless, clumsy-tender
release. I observe
the rules; cut off
here in the dimension

of pure humanity, my need for air
a limiting factor,
I look through into
your life. Its mysteries

disarm me. Turning
away a second time
to earth, to air, I leave you
to your slow-fangled order,

taking with me
more than I came for
and less. You move back into
my head. No, it does not finish here.

VI

We were horizons
of each other's consciousness. All transactions
at this distance are small,
blurred, uninsistent. Drawn

by unlikeness, I grew
like you, or dreamed I did, sharing your cautious
sideways grip on things, not to be broken,
your smokiness of blood, as kin

to dragons we guarded
in the gloom of mangrove trunks
our hoard. I crossed the limits
into alien territory. One of us

will die of this, I told myself; and one of us
did. The other

swam off to lick warm stones and sulk with clouds along a
                                                    shoreline;
regretting the deep

shelves and downward spaces,
breathing easy,
but knowing something more
was owed and would take place. I go down

in the dark to that encounter, the sun
at my back. On the sea-bed
your eyes on their sticks
click white in the flattened shadow of my head.

VII

A dreamy phosphorescence
paddles towards me. The moon drowses,
feeds, its belly white, its tough shell
black. We are afloat

together. You are
my counterweight there, I hang above you
in sunlight and a balance
is struck. No, the end

will not be like this.
We belong to different orders, and are trapped
by what we chose. Our kinship
is metaphorical, but no less deadly for all that,

old Dreadnought; as if I wore
black and carried death clenched in my fist. I do
wear black. My hand is open. It is my teeth
that seek you in the dark. And I approach bearing a death.

VIII

It was always like this: you
broken before me,
beautiful in all
the order of your parts, an anatomy lesson,

the simple continent
our bodies broke away from.
Because you are so open, because
the whole of your life

is laid out here, a chamber
to be entered and stripped. You have nothing
to hide. That sort of power
kills us, for whom

moonlight, the concept blue,
is intolerably complex as
our cells are, each an open universe
expanding beyond us, the tug

of immortality.
We shall reach it and still die.
I will be
broken after you, that was the bargain,

all this
a compact between us, who love
our privacies. I play
my part. Bent over you I dip my hand

in the bowl, I shake my cuffs, out in the open
and lost. Deep down
I am with you in the dark. The secret flesh of
my tongue enters a claw.

Because you are so open. Because you are.

IX

It is your weight
that hangs upon me. How
to deal with it. Hooded, claws locked
to your body like a star

you drag me under
the light of this occasion
to others. I've dreamed you once
too often. So this

is what it is to drown, this suffocating
torpor, giving up to
the drug of, the drag of
the moon. Here in your kingdom

I feel night harden over
my skull. That we should have come
so far out of the dark
together. I try to drown

well, I hold my breath,
no thrashing. Blue, majestic,
you blaze in my thoughts. Displacing more
than your real weight, making less

than the usual disturbance,
you plunge and take me with you.
I go out
in silence, in full view

of waiters; having learned
this much at least; to die true
to my kind—upright, smiling—
and like you, beyond speech.

X

No I am not ashamed
of our likeness, of what is in it that betrays me,
a smell of salt

backwaters, a native
grasp on the gist
of things, our local patch

of not-quite-solid earth from which the vast swing of the
sky
is trackable. Night
comes on and I am caught

with a whole life on my hands,
in my mouth raw words,
the taste of so much air, so much water,

flesh. It was never to be weighed,
this dull shore and its landscape, water
poised above water

and all its swarming creatures, against the kingdom of cloud
castles
we build with our breath
But words made you

a fact in my head. You were
myself in another species, brute
blue, a bolt of lightning, maybe God.

Now all has been made plain
between us, the weights are equal, though the sky
tilts, and the sun

with a splash I do not hear breaks into
the dark. We are one at last. Assembled here
out of earth, water, air

to a love feast. You lie open
before me. I am ready.
Begin.

An Die Musik

We might have known it always: music
is the landscape we move through in our dreams, and in
                                                    the Garden
it was music we shared
with the beasts. Even plants
unbend, are enchanted. A voice wading
adagio through air, high, clear, wordless, opens perspectives
in the deepest silence; clovers
hum; the jungle's layered
sound-mix seeks horizons, arranging itself as avenues.

What else does it make,
this *concert champetre*, if not a space we might re-enter
in innocence, pure steps
of sound on which the creatures
descend at almost dusk to recognise, as in a pool,
their names (not *cat*, not *Moggy*), and passion-flowers
incline their busy flywheels to the sun, spinning a line
of melody that modulates from yellow
to green as in mirror fugues and counter-clockwise through
                                                    the year.

So then, play your beanfield
Vivaldi's *Gloria* and see the thin pods swell, miraculous and
                                                    many
as the mouths of Hosannah. Watch them
explode across a stave, the angel syllables,
zip-fresh, sky-packed, and flutter
prestissimi on strings in hemidemisemiquavers.
Let the countryside be filled
with a din, a chime, an agricultural boom, real orchestras
(the Boston Pops) in real market gardens.

Imagine as *Ein Heldenleben* blooms
in a paddock, the slow inner lives of pumpkins, big stones
cracking, a moon-washed field

astir like a symphony as Bruckner coaxes the zucchini.
The green things of the earth
discover a fifth season to push through to, all
grace notes, as their vegetable souls
aspire to 'the condition'. A new species
taps at the boundaries. Beethoven's Tenth is what it breathes.

Ode: Stravinsky's Grave

Transposing our bodies
in grey light to the island
graveyard, we
were aware (as many

who make this water journey
are not) that intervals
of stillness and silence
are music between times

solid enough,
among mist and the marsh bird's
calling, to sustain
a man's weight, a cathedral's

centuries of shifting
from the right knee to the left.
The Campanile
ticks, a metronome

conducting the wavelets
on past lines-of-washing
tenements that hang
on a breath. The dead keep

an ear to the ground,
have time to grow accustomed
to the beat. Our senses
cannot support

such whiteness as the dome
of heaven breathes into
existence. Music gives it
colour and key,

it flows and is blue
if the day is, black,
or at night a piano-roll
punched with light and tumbling

sonatas. We stay among the dead,
observing how the twentieth century
favours the odd
conjunction and has made

strange bedfellows. (Not all of us
would rejoice at the last trump
to discover we'd been laid
by Diaghilev). The parting

bell tolls over us,
and those who can, and we
among them, re-embark.
The weather's shifted

ground so many times
in minutes, it might be
magic or miracle and you the day's
composer as you are

the century's, though at home among
immortals. We go back
the long way via the dead
silence of the Arsenal, its boom

raised, its big guns open
-mouthed before the town.
I talk to a Negro kid
from New Jersey, thinking of what

my traveller's cheques will buy
(which also work
by numbers) whoever stole them
from me—not Fame, not Love; and how

we put out crumbs to catch
birds and such scraps
of sky as are filled with
a singing; and what like Love

is not to be caught
by intent, the longer breath
of late works. A city
wades out of the dark

towards us. Our boat
falls still, steadies a moment,
then rides
in among the watery monuments.

Haystacks

The whole field stalk on stalk, scythed, gathered, stacked
in conical low-pitched ricks, loose monuments
to use and frugal plenty. A platoon of pup-tents
on hard ground, and those whose last sleep rocked
them clean out of their skins, whom midnight drank
through straws or whistled tunes on, gone through the
                                              needle's
eye these haycocks hid. They make arrangements,
with red, with mauve, with green; approach such colour
as a spyglass finds when sun with dry thatch meddles,
or acid in veins, implausible hot pink,
the tin-sheet breath that sheds throw off combusting
at noon. These bundles of antique spills imagine
a life in the field again, pitched bale, heaped barrow.
Each straw sounds with its own voice, re-enlisting
in the loud ruck of things. Bent scarlet backs
unhump and ease off indigo. In row
upon row, blond shock-heads dazzle, a world at dawn—
the one side sleet, the other sun-burst yellow.

A Place in Tuscany

In its zinc tub the basil
ventures a new leaf;
the view over this wall
is air and three turkey
-cocks under persimmons;
fantails spread, they jostle
for a place in the sun.

Women in black go hacking
greenstuff by a fence,
in their heads the name of this one
gone, that one
to come. Between
births the midwife knits
in an archway; between deaths

the coffin-maker croons,
from the same plank fashions
beds; in time these few
unchanging things assume
a village street is peopled,
as year after year and down through
the same names called

as night comes on and planets
hang, a Mars, a Venus,
between boughs, and children's places
at a table are filled,
the same fields pass. They yield
corn, wine, olives
and the scholar who weaves

their names in a crown
for the Virgin's hair. The basil

adds a new leaf
to a scene already heaped
past fullness. Dew-plumped, star
-touched, midnight is richer
for the weight of its breath.

Crows

At eighty you believe
that only a miracle
can save you. A sick
crow claws at the shutter;
you cough in sympathy.

Five centuries back,
by sympathetic magic,
Cerbone, a black
saint, cleared this valley
of crows. Today live scarecrows

troop through the grain, *Aark aark*
they creak, *a miracle!*
The sky this harvest month
is crowless, though weeping
women still wear black.

From a Time of Disruption, 1982

Lightning, a struck match:
the view leaps out
of my head, thunder claps.
I have fastened the shutters,
set saucepans for drips.

At first flash this village
severs connection
with the century and floats,
a wet flame in a saucer
set high on its shelf.

Farmers in dark kitchens
step back a day to fetch in
hay. They shake
their heads, unsteady ricks.
I dream at my desk,

candleflame approaches
its shadow, two words touch.
Later, when the link
remade, weathervane
and clock will celebrate

with creak and chime our late
re-entry to the present
and colour come back to flood
a screen, the happy concept
blue, the wet fact red.

Harvest Month

Big clouds like haystacks circle
the night. They tumble
needles all round us
in the mown field. Fireflies totter,

hot souls, impulsive fragments
of a closer universe.
We sleep, our skin sweats cornflowers,
at twelve the moon breaks in.

Somewhere downhill a lone
corncrake, set on
by its shadow in lit stubble,
incessantly, plaintively dins.

A Brief History of Tuscany

A countryside pieced out
in small tasks: salad plucked
among weeds, after a cloudburst
along sun-spiked hedge and highway
rainbows, buckets of snails.

Each jigsaw-plot the table
where a family eats twice daily,
the live hands and the ghostly;
in the long view this province
a string of such meals.

Magpie

I

borrows and lends a voice to what he filches:
garden, all smash, is apples again, glass catches
a breath, stray bone, bent fork and teacup handle
—twigs of a match-and-marry dialect.

Magpie changes the subject, takes things out
of themselves into second nature. Necklace, roundel
of dead stones, buds a stalk; teaspoon, a hacked
apostle, hangs honey-mouthed, ringed round with
                                                sunlight.

II

Magpie stays close to home, is at home
in one field, maybe two, in all seasons.
His slick head swivels, flick-knives a glare; the day's
transformed: two spoons, a chipped glass ring—
                                    O Woolworths!

*It would take more than one lifetime
to ornament this heath,* he croaks, *with all
a single life affords. Let swallows husband
their small heat in flocks and freight it south,*

*It'll stick. I set a lure to catch companions—
a tie-pin, this flashy plume. To see one magpie
is ill luck. A mirror makes us two:
two quick fires, one the sun, in a wet furrow.*

III

Snowfall, white noise:
no peacock blue
toque or silk scarlet
in the blank field, no brassy
jangling of tongues.

Still I would make,
says magpie, *this treat*
for the sun. I speak
green and I bring
a thief's pack of glitters,

let common things shine
in the brute air, too cheap
to number. My feathers,
this false jewel, this mirror,
are part of the scene.

IV

Peach, apricot, berry—
earth and the sun
between them concoct

occasions, hang bush
and bough with their gaudery.
In the light of such tinkering,

says magpie, *spoons*
have a place; so do mirrors.
I hoard them, I hang them

in thickets where they double
the sun; weekdays are brighter,
my song too is brighter.

For all his adherence
to plain sound, magpie keeps
touch with the ado

he springs from: this world,
this only, and its twin
and rival—This World II.

V

When magpie's head pokes through
a break in the weather,
his eye, that chink
in blacker-than-black,
gives nothing away
with his gimcrack glare of what's
within: God's
lumber, trash and treasure.

When magpie stares
at a blank field he colours
it in, he hails up
high jinks: from two
spoons strikes up a jig,
from handbags tossed
in a ditch a whole soap-opera
in code, flick-flacked from mirrors.

VI

Among the day's odd bits
of plunder, plastic hair-clip,
ivory tower
of a game lost in the grass,
magpie looks up

astonished. What's this?
Round, smooth, complete
and sealed, it belongs
if at all to a new order
—a stone with a pulse-beat.

The stone cracks open, wings
shell off the sky,
this first one, and break
into blue. *This too,*
says magpie, *is a way*

of making it new, sans
mirrors, sans *bric-à-brac.*
The thing is
and can't be changed, its call-sign
ugly-my-own creak creak.

Pentecostal

Lit scales in the grass, in a dented pail soft guts
that spill their lost light thin as the Pleiades.
Mullet, whiting, bream—the terror of Fridays
their names, their boneless ghosts lodged in my throat.
Beyond the incinerator: slow-travelling comets
silver a wet path: fat snails like wagon
-wheels out pioneering our heat-struck, hushed
-after -hail backyard embayment, caught in the open
in a smash of sunflower-stalks. Gelatinous thick
tongues in a shell too far from the sea, they thunder
Te Deums to table-salt, writhe in the anguished
hiss of deliquescence. I make myself small,
then smaller; approach the vanishing-point; surrender
breath then blood to hear from the wet sizzle
of flesh made dung, scoured shell, sucked bone, their clear
death-aria in my throat, voice of the word
-less creature in us that rages against hook,
against withering salt, against frying-pan or fire.

Familiar Story

A sidereal station-wagon, sleepy twins
in the back, their dark heads bent over a tale
I never heard the end of. For which of us
was this star accidental? I spoke to him
in our local tongue; he smiled, he did not speak.
Each word I learned for the new world deafened me
to his perfect silences, till the thump
in my head of early thunder fitted itself
to the mutterings of that couple, shag-haired,
                              dewlapped,
who breathed over my bed, shuffled a broom
at dawn among cooking-pots, in nightmares stroked
my skin and kept me human. I took their name,
and learned to recognise in their clack and jabber
such beasts as when I called them lifted their gaze
towards me, in clouds of sour-straw breath hulked in
to be yoked. What names they bore when he called to
                              them
I never knew, or in what shape they came
like poems to lick the strange salt from his hands.

Vocation

A minor form of praying: big hands plump
the dough, invoke domestic saints that gravely
watch over a task, will maybe raise it—
the pumpkins also raised; green thumbs push down
a seed and shift the earth. By the same process
of small-talk over growing things new cousins
occurred in aunts and households safe as houses
broke up as hatchet murders. Out of the cloud-shop
of whisks and mixing bowls, the angels willing,
a task becomes a gift, workable magic
that a child picks up by eavesdropping, mis-hearing, mis-
remembering. It happens while we change
from foot to bare foot watching the smacked sun go
for six over a fence, then back with daylight
to brood over a bud. Slow pupils learn
by accident an art they do not know
they're already practising. One day, from days
gone under, blown brassy trumpets raise the yard.

Nostalgie

On my heels among canna-stems, in the little India
of under-our-backyard-steps. I suck on cake
-crumbed fingers, sweet mud-chocolate, dropped and the
                                                    sweeter
for it, snatched back again, dusted with earth.
'Don't *fuss*,' the old wives crooned, 'he'll swallow a peck
of that before he's done, a few grains more
won't hurt him.' They didn't, they never have; I'm still
eating. Useful so early on to get
acquainted and take no harm from it, the angel
who comes to us in so many forms, warm sandpile
Eden, new world city, all we inherit
of dirt that balls in a sweaty palm, the crust
and daily dross and excrement, the golden
muck, and will be there in our mouths when breath,
that ghostly wafer, is gone—last taste
on the tongue of what came first and madeleine
to the rest: to savour which, illuminate crumb
by crumb, will take at least another lifetime.

Hemisphere

The talk after dark is of sunflowers
in their season big as dinner-plates. Outside,
the deep woods of North America
are preparing for snow, its weight unfallen
light along their boughs, the only bird
today the stone my arm sent flying
across ice, its mimic twitter. Down below,
where mind moves quick
in its other hemisphere,
the big plates, all light, are coming out
in kitchens: breakfast time. The two rooms touch
and balance a moment, sunflower-heads
that might at another time or in another life be owls.
They climb over a white picket fence
to confound us, these agents of two worlds.

Earth Tremor, Yaddo, NY, 1988

In the round mouth of a wineglass
a tongue swings silent, light
-rings crash. It is the earth
reminding us, in a stilled breath, what it is
to be still; that we are not.

If a stone had consciousness,
said Spinoza, *would it not*
believe when I let it fly that it was flying?
and Schopenhauer: *Add only*
that the stone would be right.

Collected Poems

LES MURRAY

Les Murray is universally regarded as Australia's greatest poet. To understand why, one need look no further than this *Collected Poems*. It is a magnificent book, revealing every conceivable resource of language and poetic form, full of humour and humanity, rich in detailed observation, and studded with profound perceptions of natural and spiritual truth.

No poet has attempted a wider range of subjects, from the life of Australian country people to the cities of the world, from the distant and recent past to the present and the future, from the microscopic scale to that of galaxies. More remarkably, no poet has been so consistently successful in such a variety of genres, from epigram to epic.

This collection comprises all of the poetry which Les Murray wishes to preserve, apart from the verse-novel *The Boys Who Stole the Funeral* and his current collection *Dog Fox Field*. It makes the sequence 'The Idyll Wheel', which appeared as a limited edition in 1989, generally available for the first time.

Collected Poems

ROSEMARY DOBSON

Rosemary Dobson's *Collected Poems* brings together almost two hundred poems written over a period of fifty years. The book will be one of the abiding joys of Australian literature, a lifework of love and dedication to the craft of writing. It presents the poet's work as a whole and shows the progress and the diversity of her art, so often characterised by wit and irony.

Many of the poems are close to epistles or letters. They belong to this world, its people and events. They surprise, however, with their weight of feeling and nervous insight, and with what James McAuley wrote of as this poet's 'sense of a mystery . . . momentarily glimpsed'.

Rosemary Dobson's style with its spare, clean and hard qualities is European in its emphases. Yet she has been subtle and sensitive in her awareness of Australia as her place of belonging. She has shared with Judith Wright, A. D. Hope, James McAuley, David Campbell and Les Murray a pre-eminence among modern Australian poets. Her strong recent development in the 1980s and her perseverance as an artist reveal a classical sense of tradition that is open to change and the future.

Beauty is the Straw

AMY WITTING

Amy Witting is an intelligent poet, fully the equal of the brightest anywhere. The fact is proved not least by her never forgetting that a poem must also move us. A poet of reserve and a genuine independence of mind, she has been slow to attract attention, in part because she has not anxiously sought it. Discerning readers, however, have been amazed that so fine a poet could have been working unnoticed at such a level of achievement. Her wise, richly honest conversations with people and with experience itself welcome the thoughtful readers, and mark a talent we can confidently call major.

Orpheus

A. D. HOPE

As he approaches the end of a distinguished career, the elder statesman of Australian poetry is writing as well as ever. Yet even the most fervent of A. D. Hope's admirers will be astonished by the range and power of this latest collection of his work, which is published in his 85th year.

Though several of these poems face the sad truth of bodily disintegration, they do so cheerfully, with ironic wit rather than with morbidity. Other poems deal just as wittily with Hope's familiar theme of carnal love, most notably in the rollicking bawdy ballad 'Teaser rams'.

The sequence 'Western Elegies', at the beginning of the book, touches on all of Hope's major concerns — love and language and mortality — and is moreover a revolutionary technical departure. It is the work of a master, still at the height of his powers.

Confessions of a Corinthian

JULIAN CROFT

The name of ancient Corinth was for centuries a synonym for luxury and self-indulgence. By rebelling against what he saw as a paralysed and parochial Australia of his youth, the poet Julian Croft now considers that he helped to create a pervasive Corinth in Australia, one in which the slow erosion of values in the small towns of our east coast horrifies him as much as the excesses of Surfers Paradise. In coming to terms with how we create consciousness, and his part in creating a crummy one, he explores the past in Proustian detail, and examines the latest insights of a human-centred theory of physics. The poetry in which he deals with all of these concerns maintains the verve and feeling familiar from his celebrated earlier collection *Breakfast in Shanghai.*